TEN ANIMALS IN ANTARCTICA

A Counting Book

MOIRA COURT

 Charlesbridge

Antarctica is the coldest, windiest, driest continent in the world.

SOUTH POLE

In Antarctica, there are icy deserts,
mountain ranges, and volcanoes—
some buried deep under the ice.

Antarctica is home to some
amazing and unique animals.
How many can you count?

One freckled, speckled leopard seal

sailing on an icy-blue berg.

Two courtly, portly **emperor penguins**
waddling across the polar plains.

3 Three lumbersome, cumbersome southern

elephant seals lining the sandy shore.

Four slow-paced, big-faced southern right whales

wallowing in rippling reflections.

4

Five speedy, beady-eyed snow petrels
somersaulting by craggy cliffs.

Six cheeky, sneaky **orcas** surveying the frosty floes.

7 Seven inky, slinky Antarctic flying squid

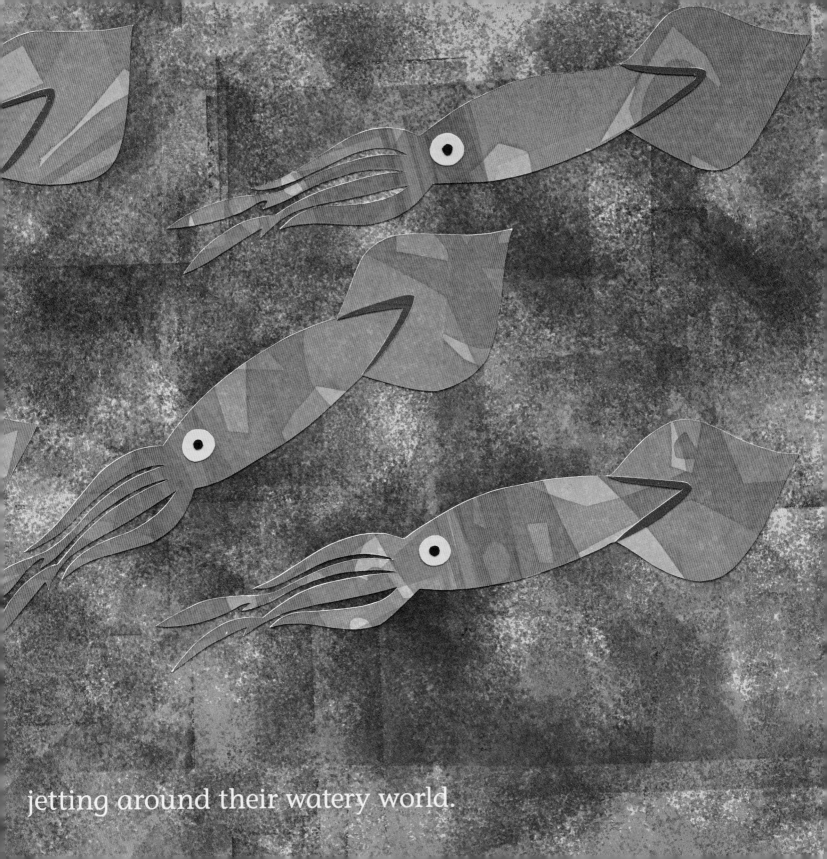

jetting around their watery world.

Eight shrimpish, pinkish Antarctic krill

drifting with the turning tide.

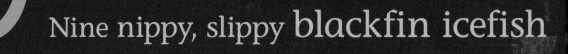

9

Nine nippy, slippy blackfin icefish

haunting the dusky depths.

Ten crimson, vermilion sea stars
creeping about on twinkle toes.

One to ten!

This wonderful group of quirky creatures
thrives at the very bottom of the world
in the harshest weather.

ABOUT ANTARCTICA

Antarctica is the southernmost continent on Earth. It covers 5.4 million square miles (14 million square kilometers), which is nearly one and a half times the size of the United States. Antarctica is almost completely covered in ice, which can be almost 3 miles (5 kilometers) thick. The average temperature during the coldest time of year is −81°F (−63°C), and the lowest temperature ever recorded there (and anywhere on Earth) was a bone-chilling −128.6°F (−89.2°C). Antarctica gets hardly any rain or snow, but it does have very strong winds, with recorded speeds up to 200 miles (322 kilometers) per hour.

The South Pole is in Antarctica. There is actually more than one South Pole, though. In fact, there are several!

The Ceremonial South Pole is near  the research facility called Amundsen-Scott South Pole Station. It's a stout red-and-white striped pole topped with a fancy, shiny metal ball. It is surrounded by the flags of the twelve governments that signed the original Antarctic Treaty on December 1, 1959: Argentina, Australia, Belgium, Chile, France, Japan, New Zealand, Norway, South Africa, the Soviet Union (now Russia), the United Kingdom, and the United States. All these countries (and more since 1959) have agreed that Antarctica should be preserved for scientific research and that no one country should claim it as their own.

The Geographic South Pole

is the "real" South Pole. It's very close to the ceremonial pole, is the southernmost place in the world, and is one end of Earth's axis. The sign that marks its location is relocated each year because the ice moves!

There is also the **Magnetic South Pole**, which is where compasses point when indicating south; the Southern Pole of Inaccessibility, which is the farthest point in Antarctica from any coastline; and the Southern Pole of Cold, the coldest place on Earth. You could look them up to learn more!

ABOUT THE ANIMALS

Leopard seals are not only spotted like leopards; they also are just as fierce. They prey on penguins and smaller seals, catching them in their big mouth with their long, sharp teeth. They are solitary animals, spending most of their lives alone, often on ice.

Southern elephant seals are named after the male's snout, which looks like an elephant's trunk. They are the largest of all seals; males can grow up to 20 feet (6 meters) long and weigh four tons (3.6 metric tons)—that's about the same as two cars! Despite being clumsy on land, southern elephant seals are excellent swimmers and can stay underwater for two hours and go almost a mile (1.6 kilometers) deep.

Emperor penguins are the largest and toughest of all penguins. They are the only animal that lives on the open ice of Antarctica during the winter. Emperor penguins sometimes walk 50 miles (80 kilometers) or more across the ice to feed in the ocean.

Southern right whales are leisurely swimmers. They have white growths called callosities on their enormous heads. Callosities are home to whale barnacles, parasitic worms, and whale lice. They form a unique pattern that stays the same over the whale's lifetime.

Snow petrels are acrobatic aeronauts, swooping, soaring, and plummeting at speeds of up to 25 miles (40 kilometers) per hour. They make their nests on ledges and in crevices of high cliffs, and they produce a stinky stomach oil that they can spray from their mouth to keep trespassers away.

Orcas, also called killer whales, are the largest members of the dolphin family. They are among the most intelligent of all animals and are fast learners that can pass on knowledge to other pod members, working as a team to hunt prey. These crafty creatures use echolocation—bouncing sound off objects to find them—for navigation and hunting. They often swim around and under ice floes.

Antarctic flying squid squirt a black substance we call ink when they're frightened. It spreads into a dark cloud that confuses predators—while the squid whizzes away.

Antarctic krill are 2 inches (5 centimeters) long and live in huge swarms of up to 30,000 individuals. Krill have an exoskeleton—a skeleton on the outside of their body. They are on the menu for penguins, seals, and whales.

Blackfin icefish are toothy fish that have skin rather than scales. They produce a natural antifreeze in their body, which keeps ice from forming in their blood. The adults live at the bottom of the ocean.

Sea stars have tube feet, an eyespot at the end of each arm, two stomachs, and a mouth in the middle of their underside. They eat anything they can find, and they move around underwater to find food.

For faraway Tilde and my inspirational Winnie—M. C.

2021 First US edition

At the time of publication, all URLs printed in this book were
accurate and active. Charlesbridge and the author are not
responsible for the content or accessibility of any website.

Published by Charlesbridge
9 Galen Street
Watertown, MA 02472
(617) 926-0329
www.charlesbridge.com

Original edition first published by Fremantle Press,
Western Australia, in 2019 as *Antarctica*.

Library of Congress Cataloging-in-Publication Data
Names: Court, Moira, author, illustrator.
Title: Ten animals in Antarctica: a counting book / Moira Court.
Other titles: Antarctica
Description: First US edition. | Watertown, MA: Charlesbridge,
    2021. | "Original edition first published by Fremantle Press,
    Western Australia, in 2019 as *Antarctica*." | Summary:
    "Antarctica is the coldest, windiest, driest continent in the
    world, with icy deserts, mountain ranges, and volcanoes—
    some buried deep under the ice. Antarctica is home to some
    amazing and unique animals. How many can you count?"—
    Provided by publisher.
Identifiers: LCCN 2019050929 (print) | LCCN 2019050930
    (ebook) | ISBN 9781623542320 (hardcover) | ISBN
    9781632899996 (ebook)
Subjects: LCSH: Animals—Antarctica—Juvenile literature. |
    Counting—Juvenile literature. | Antarctica—Juvenile literature.
    | LCGFT: Picture books.
Classification: LCC QL106 .C68 2021 (print) | LCC QL106
    (ebook) | DDC 591.9989—dc23
LC record available at https://lccn.loc.gov/2019050929
LC ebook record available at https://lccn.loc.gov/2019050930

Printed in China
(hc) 10 9 8 7 6 5 4 3 2 1

Illustrations done in printmaking and collage
Display type set in Papercute by Julien Saurin
Text type set in Stone Informal by Adobe Systems
Printed by 1010 Printing International Limited
    in Huizhou, Guangdong, China
Production supervision by Brian G. Walker
Designed by Cathleen Schaad